It's All About Energy

Written by Keith Pigdon

Series Consultant: Linda Hoyt

WorldWise™
Content-based Learning

Contents

Introduction

Every time you turn on a light or the heating in your house, every time you make a phone call, and every time you go somewhere in a car, bus, train or plane, you use energy.

The use of energy is growing quickly because the number of people on Earth is also growing very quickly – in the last 50 years the earth's population has doubled. Because of this, more energy is being used.

Most of our energy comes from fossil fuels – oil, natural gas, coal. These energy sources are warming the planet and making serious changes to the environment.

But there are other sources of energy that do not damage our planet and will never run out – sun, wind and water.

World population milestones

1 billion	2 billion	3 billion	4 billion	5 billion	6 billion	7 billion	8 billion
1804	1927	1960	1974	1987	1999	2011	2023

Since 1987, the world population has been growing by 1 billion every 12 years.

Find out more

Look at these photos. All these things use electricity. Over two days, make a list of everything you use that requires electricity.

Chapter 1

Where does our energy come from?

Much of the energy that we personally use is in the form of electricity.

Coal, oil or natural gas are the main fuels used to generate electricity. They are all fossil fuels. About 85 per cent of the world's energy comes from burning fossil fuels. The rest comes from different kinds of **renewable** fuels.

Where do fossil fuels come from?

Fossil fuels come from deep under the ground. Coal, oil (petroleum) and natural gas are called fossil fuels because they were formed hundreds of millions of years ago from dead plants and animals. Because fossil fuels take millions of years to form, they cannot be replaced once we have used them. They are known as **non-renewable** energy sources.

← oil

Oil companies drill deep down into the ground to get oil.

Fossil fuels

Oil, coal and natural gas are the most frequently used fossil fuels. At this time, they are a cheaper source of power, compared with most renewables, but over time, this will almost certainly change.

Oil

How important is it as an energy source?
- Oil is the most widely used fossil fuel.
- 33% of our energy comes from oil.

How do we use it?
- Oil is used to make fuel for cars and other forms of transport.

How do we get it?
- Oil is found deep under the earth's surface.
- Oil companies drill into the earth's crust, through rocks, sand, water and other material, to reach the oil, which they then pump to the surface.

How does our use of oil harm the earth?
- Burning oil increases global warming.
- There is an increased danger of water pollution.

Coal

How important is it as an energy source?
- Coal is the major fuel for making electricity.
- 40% of electricity comes from coal.

How do we use it?
- Power stations burn coal to generate electricity.
- Coal is used in the production of steel, concrete and paper.

How do we get it?
- Coal is also found deep under the earth's surface.
- Mining companies dig deep mines or large open-cut mines to reach the coal.

How does our use of coal harm the earth?
- Burning coal increases global warming.
- Coal is the most polluting fossil fuel.

Natural gas

How important is it as an energy source?
- About 24% of our energy comes from natural gas.

How do we use it?
- Natural gas is used for heating.
- It is also used in power stations to generate electricity.

How do we get it?
- Natural gas is also found deep under the earth's surface.
- Gas companies drill into the earth's crust, through rocks, sand, water and other material, to access the gas.

How does our use of natural gas harm the earth?
- Natural gas is the cleanest fossil fuel to burn, but it still contributes to global warming.

Chapter 2

Fossil fuels and the environment

When we burn fossil fuels to make energy, gases and very tiny pieces of coal ash are released into the air. These solid pieces of ash and gases harm the environment in many ways. They can pollute both the air and the water, and this can cause damage to all living things.

Pollution changes our environment in many harmful ways.

▼ Beijing, China, on a clear day (below left) and a smoggy day (below right)

Smog from burning fossil fuels

Smog is formed when the fumes and tiny solid pieces such as **carbon** from factories, electricity plants, cars and other transport mixes with fog. On smoggy days, when there is no wind, a thick brown film can be seen over a city for a day, a week or longer. Some cities are known for their high levels of smog. People are often warned to stay inside when smog is very thick. Smog can cause coughing, throat and chest infections, and start **asthma** attacks.

Find out more

What are the smoggiest cities in the world?

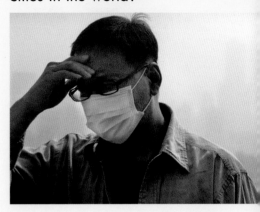

What is acid rain?

Gases released from factories and cars that use energy by burning fossil fuels are carried up into the **atmosphere**. The gases combine with water droplets to form acids. This creates acid rain that destroys plants, pollutes water sources and **erodes** buildings.

Acid rain harms fish and wildlife in streams, lakes and marshes. It also flows through the soil and can harm many living things in **ecosystems** that cannot live with high acid levels. Dead or dying trees or even forests are a common sight in areas where acid rain is a problem. Acid rain can also damage walls, roofs and other building materials.

This forest has been destroyed by acid rain.

Acid rain and our environment

1 Acidic gases are released into the atmosphere.

2 Gases are carried upward by the wind.

3 Gases combine with water droplets to form acids.

4 Acid rain falls.

5 Acid rain destroys plants and pollutes water sources.

How harmful is global warming?

The majority of scientists agree that the earth is warming quickly and that weather patterns are changing around the world. They also agree that human activities have caused this increase. The changes in climate caused by the activity of humans is called global warming.

In the past, Earth has gone through periods of being cooler and warmer, but these changes took place very slowly over many thousands of years.

Today, Earth is warming much faster than ever before. Over the past 50 years, the release of harmful gases into the atmosphere has increased rapidly. As we use more energy, we burn more fossil fuels. Also, we are cutting down forests and clearing land for cities and towns. This is harmful. Forests remove **carbon dioxide** from the air and release **oxygen**.

Effects of global warming

Environment/Society	Impact
Warmer, drier summers	Less rain and droughts in some areas
Warmer, wetter winters	More rain in some areas Storms, cyclones and other severe weather events leading to flooding and damage to buildings and crops
Melting ice caps and glaciers	Rising sea levels lead to floods and habitat destruction. Polar bears under threat from melting ice caps
Expanding sea levels	As water gets warmer, it expands and sea levels rise. Some islands and low-lying coastal places are under threat from flooding as sea levels rise. Oceans become more acidic and marine animals are harmed.
Health	Increase in heat-related deaths Ticks and mosquitoes increase in number and spread diseases.
Ecosystems	Changes to land and sea-based ecosystems These can cause problems with the food and water that humans and other living things depend on.

Chapter 3

How can we solve our energy problems?

We can solve our energy problems if we reduce the amount of fossil fuels we burn. We are already taking action to reduce the amount of fossil fuels being burned, but at the moment, 85 per cent of energy still comes from fossil fuels.

Use less energy

We should try to choose products that use less energy. The car industry makes cars that use much less fuel than the cars we drove in the past. Many modern appliances and lights use less energy, and some people take more care about how much electricity they use.

Use renewables

The sun, wind, water and the heat of the earth are sources of **renewable** energy. These renewables make up a growing part of our energy resources. Of these, hydro-electric power is used in many countries and is still the main source of renewable power. Hydropower makes no gas or other pollutants and is always available if there is enough water.

	How it works	Advantages	Disadvantages
Wind	On a wind farm, the wind turns blades on turbines, which creates electrical energy	Clean Plentiful supply in windy places	Wind not blowing all the time Some people don't like the look or the noise
Sun	Solar panels use the energy of the sun to make electricity	Clean Plentiful supply Can be used in your own home Can be used on a large scale	No electricity made at night Sunlight varies in different parts of the world
Water	The energy from water in fast-flowing rivers is captured and turned into electricity known as hydro-electricity	Clean Plentiful supply Low running costs	Needs sufficient rainfall or a reliable river
Heat from the earth	Heat and steam under the earth's surface are used to make geothermal energy	Produces little pollution Plentiful supply in some places	Not available in many places Heat needs to be near the earth's surface

Wind power

A wind farm, Albany, Western Australia

Wind power is clean and plentiful. The use of wind power has grown very quickly in many countries where wind farms have been built on land and in the ocean. Today, wind farms are able to store electricity in huge banks of batteries for use when there is not enough wind.

Some smaller towns are now getting most of their electricity from wind farms. A wind farm in Greensburg, Kansas, USA, generates more electricity than the town of 785 people needs. The excess is sold off to other energy companies. Since 2001, Albany in Western Australia has had a wind farm that generates about 50 per cent of the town's electricity. Albany has a population of 37,399 people.

The three largest producers of wind energy in 2017

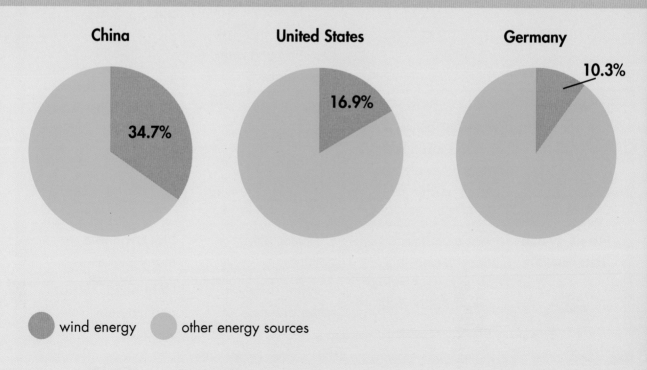

China
34.7%

United States
16.9%

Germany
10.3%

wind energy   other energy sources

Some countries are now using wind power to generate a greater percentage of their electricity. Wind power's share of worldwide electricity usage at the start of 2017, however, was four per cent.

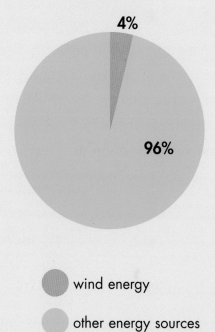

Electricity from wind energy, 2017

4%

96%

⬤ wind energy

⬤ other energy sources

Find out more

How do communities decide on the best place to build wind farms?

A wind farm is a group of wind turbines in the same place that are linked together to make electricity.

Wind power in Australia

Wind power has grown quickly from small beginnings in Australia. Wind power now matches hydro-electricity as Australia's greatest producer of renewable energy. South Australia and Victoria are the leading states, but many wind farms are being built in other states and territories.

In Australia, wind farms have been built on farming land. Farmers receive money from the owners of the wind farms for the use of their land for giant wind turbines. Farmers are able to continue farming their land.

Farmers who receive this money are happy about having these giant turbines on their properties, but some farmers from nearby farms who don't get paid may be disappointed. In the wider community there are people who are strongly opposed to wind farms. Some who live close to them say that the turbines make them ill, some complain about the noise and others dislike the look of wind farms.

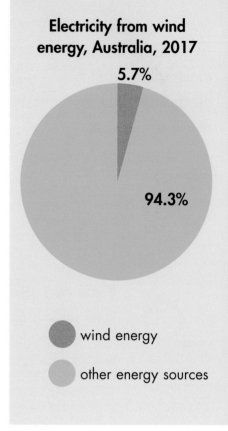

Electricity from wind energy, Australia, 2017

5.7%

94.3%

● wind energy

● other energy sources

Wind turbines on farmland in Victoria

World's Largest Battery

1 December 2017

The Hornsdale Power Reserve, containing the world's largest lithium-ion battery, was launched today in South Australia. The Power Reserve is connected to the Hornsdale Wind Farm.

Clean, affordable wind energy can now be sent to Australia's energy grid 24 hours a day, as required. The stored energy in the Power Reserve is available to the South Australian government for emergency situations. The Power Reserve provides instant supply to the grid while other backup devices such as gas-fired generators are started up.

ENERGY ⚡ STORAGE

Wind farms are often criticised for only being able to provide power when the wind blows and having to shutdown in extreme winds. This development shows how, with the aid of storage, they can help to stabilise the energy supply.

Solar power

Solar electricity is pollution-free and has the advantage that people can get electricity from solar panels on the roofs of their houses. This means that where there is enough sunshine and the roof of the house is not shaded, people can produce clean, green energy and reduce **greenhouse gases** themselves.

In winter, less energy is produced and, of course, no energy is produced at night. But in spring, summer and autumn, solar panels give excellent results. Hot water can also be made from solar energy.

▼ This solar power plant is in China. China has the world's largest solar power plants.

22

Some countries are very keen to reduce the amount of fossil fuels they burn. Their governments have helped people install rooftop solar systems by paying them for the electricity they create but don't need. This means that electricity is fed into the main **power grid** for others to use. This happens on sunny days when a house with solar panels cannot use all the energy it generates.

Large batteries that can store solar power for later use are now available for home use and will increasingly give more people reasons to use solar panels.

Large scale solar and batteries

The 220 Bungala Solar Farm is located near Port Augusta in South Australia. Once completed, it will be Australia's largest solar farm, generating enough electricity to power 82,000 Australian households. 1.2 million solar panels will power these households. The plant will have a battery storage system.

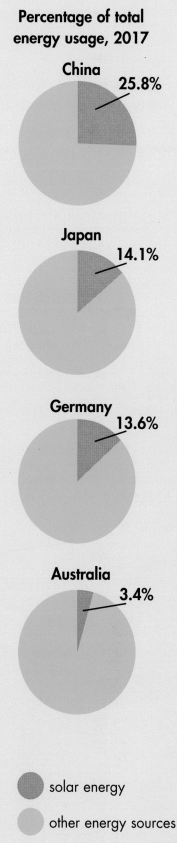

Percentage of total energy usage, 2017

China
25.8%

Japan
14.1%

Germany
13.6%

Australia
3.4%

○ solar energy

○ other energy sources

How can we solve our energy problems?

Solar power in Australia

Solar power has also grown quickly in Australia. Small rooftop systems of solar panels that are connected to the national electricity grid are seen throughout Australia. South Australia leads the way in household rooftop solar panels.

Many major public buildings and several hundred public schools also have rooftop solar.

Did you know?
In 2011, solar panels were installed on Parliament House in Canberra.

Find out more
What percentage of houses in your state or territory has rooftop solar panels?

Many houses in Australia have solar panels.

A bright idea

A group of university students had an idea to save money on their electricity bills and to do something for the environment. Could they get all their electricity from solar power? They decided to give it a go.

They put solar panels on the roof of their apartment building, called Stucco, in Newtown, Sydney. The panels were connected to storage batteries, and each apartment could get their electricity from the batteries.

This project became Australia's first solar+battery storage apartments. Solar power produces 85 per cent of their electricity, and the students now enjoy lower power bills. Their bright idea worked.

Stucco Housing Co-operative	
Solar panels	114
Batteries	36
Residents	40
Apartments	8
Savings per month	$35

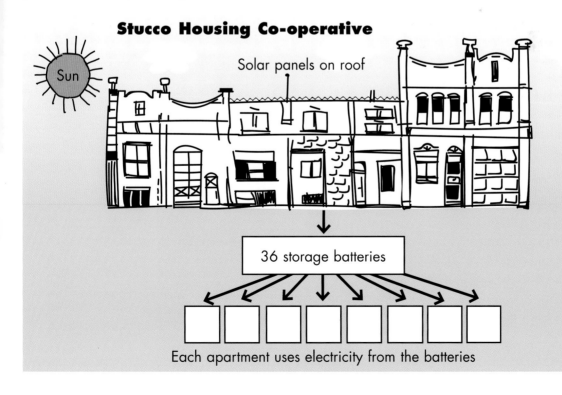

Stucco Housing Co-operative

Sun

Solar panels on roof

36 storage batteries

Each apartment uses electricity from the batteries

Hydropower in Australia

Hydro-electricity is the most widely used renewable energy source in Australia. There are more than 120 hydropower plants. Most of them are in New South Wales, Victoria and Tasmania, where there is high rainfall. The Snowy Mountains Hydro Scheme in New South Wales is the largest.

Tasmania leads the nation in renewable energy. In some years, this island state creates 93 per cent of its electricity from renewables. The major source of renewable energy in Tasmania is its extensive network of hydro-electricity stations, with some wind and small solar input. In some years, lower rainfall reduces the amount of hydro-electricity generated. Tasmania also has the lowest **carbon** emissions per person of the Australian states.

Australia gets 17 per cent of its energy from renewable sources. The other 83 per cent comes from fossil fuels. This table shows how much energy comes from renewable sources in each state and territory.

State / Territory	Renewables
Northern Territory	4%
Queensland	8%
New South Wales	11%
Western Australia	14%
Victoria	16%
Australian Capital Territory	22%
Tasmania	88%

Tasmania and the Australian government are making plans to increase renewable energy by introducing pumped storage hydro. Fourteen hydropower stations are being considered for this upgrade.

In pumped storage hydro, water that has been used to create electricity is pumped from a lower reservoir into a higher reservoir. This can be done at times when less expensive electricity from wind or solar power is available. This water is then dropped again through the turbine to create electricity.

There can be many issues involved in developing clean energy projects. People from all over Australia were opposed to the damming of rivers in Tasmania and the destruction of wilderness that took place during the construction of the dams.

◄ Jindabyne Dam. Lake Jindabyne in the Snowy Mountains has been dammed as a part of the Snowy Mountains Hydro-electric scheme.

◄ The Gordon Dam at Lake Pedder, Tasmania

Jindabyne Lake, NSW

Lake Pedder, Tasmania

What can you do?

The warming of the earth has become so problematic that many countries, governments and interest groups are trying to find solutions. Everyone can help. You, too, can help by looking through these lists and finding small changes that will make a difference.

Here are some ideas you can use to cut down on energy use.

Use less electricity

Saving electricity in your house

Switch appliances off at the power point when they are no longer being used. They use power in standby mode.

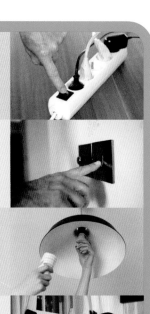

Turn off lights, computers, televisions and other appliances when they are not in use.

Use low-energy globes in your home lights. **LEDs** use very little energy.

Pull back curtains on sunny winter days and let the sun in to save on electric or gas heating.

Close the doors of rooms where heaters are on to stop heat from escaping.

Wear layers of warm clothes to keep warm instead of turning on the heater.

Recycle

Saving electricity and waste by recycling	Use rechargeable batteries instead of ordinary batteries that may leak toxic metals when thrown away.	
	Bring your food and drinks to school in reusable containers instead of plastic wrapping.	
	Create your own vegetable patch and enjoy seeing your own fruits and vegetables grow.	
	Set up a compost bin and worm farm – then you can recycle food scraps and make fertiliser for your garden.	
	Set up bins in the classroom to allow students to sort rubbish and other materials.	
	Use recycled paper where possible.	

Conclusion

There are two powerful reasons to reduce the amount of energy we use and to change to **renewable** energy.

- Fossil fuels are becoming harder and more expensive to extract from the earth. They will run out at some time in the future, though nobody knows exactly when.

- Because of the harm caused by using fossil fuels, we are likely to destroy the **atmosphere** and the environment that supports all the living things on the earth.

We know that we can change what we are doing. We can reduce the energy we use now and gradually switch over to renewable sources of energy. We can help our environment stay in a healthy state for all living things.

Glossary

asthma a life-threatening, allergic reaction that causes difficulty in breathing

atmosphere the blanket of gases that surrounds the earth

carbon a chemical found in coal, oil and natural gas that is released when these fuels are burned; it can also be found in soot and smog

carbon dioxide a colourless, odourless gas formed when carbon and oxygen are combined

ecosystem a community of living things that interact with each other and the place they live

erodes to eat away the surface of buildings

greenhouse gases gases, such as carbon dioxide, that contribute to the warming of the earth called the greenhouse effect

LED a type of energy-efficient lighting; it is an acronym for "Light Emitting Diode"

non-renewable a natural source of energy that once completely used up cannot be made again

oxygen a colourless, odourless gas found in the air, that humans and other animals need to breathe

power grid the system of wires that transfers electricity from power stations to places where it can be used

renewable a source of energy that can be replaced and therefore will never be used up

Index